Published in 2002 by Caxton Editions
20 Bloomsbury Street
London WC1B 3JH
a member of the Caxton Publishing Group

© 2002 Caxton Publishing Group

Designed and produced for Caxton Editions
by Open Door Limited
Langham, Rutland
Editing: Mary Morton and Colin Shearing
Illustration: Kevin Doyle

All rights reserved. No part of this publication may be reproduced
or transmitted in any form or by any means, electronic or
mechanical, including photocopying, recording or any information
storage and retrieval system, without prior permission in writing
from the copyright owner.

Title: Cancer
ISBN: 1 84067 488 1

SUN & MOON SIGNS

CANCER

James Petulengro

CAXTON EDITIONS

CANCER
CONTENTS

INTRODUCTION

6

SUN SIGNS ~ WHAT ARE THEY?

10

MOON SIGNS ~ WHAT ARE THEY?

12

THE SUN SIGN OF CANCER

14

CANCER
CONTENTS

THE 12 MOON SIGNS

36

CANCER SUN AND

THE 12 MOON SIGN COMBINATIONS

62

EPILOGUE

80

CANCER
INTRODUCTION

The art and science of astrology has been around for over 5,000 years and is still used by many people for many different purposes. The scientific aspect of the subject is in the astronomical calculations required to make a birth chart. A birth chart (horoscope) is like a photographic image of the planets in the sky above you when you are born. No two people in the world have the same birth chart; it is totally unique to you and is what defines your individuality. You may have many things in common with other people, but the complete birth chart is yours and yours alone. The artistic aspect of the subject is in the interpretation of the position of these planetary bodies. In this book we shall be looking particularly at the positions of the Sun and the Moon at the time of your birth and how these affect your life.

Introduction

You may find that if you were born from the 19th to the 23rd of the month your Sun sign is what is called "on the cusp". Each year the Sun enters the various Sun signs on different days so just because you were born on the 21st of the month, for example, does not necessarily mean you are the Sun sign you think you are. Calculating your birth chart will help you to discover exactly what your Sun sign is.

As a special feature, if you do not have one already, you can calculate your own birth chart including a short 8-page interpretation on my website at http://www.jamespetulengro.co.uk type in your birth details and you can then print out astrological details and your birth chart. This may also help you when you come to look at the Moon sign part of this book and the Sun and Moon combinations if you do not know your Moon sign.

Introduction

The 12 Zodiac signs are traditionally formed into four groups within which they interact and complement each other.

The first group are the elements. These consist of fire signs, earth signs, air signs and water signs. The fire signs are by nature enthusiastic and comprise Aries, Leo and Sagittarius. The Earth signs are Taurus, Virgo and Capricorn and are practical. The Air signs are Gemini, Libra and Aquarius and are intellectual. The Water signs are Cancer, Scorpio and Pisces which are emotional.

A second group is known as the qualities. The cardinal signs are Aries, Cancer, Libra and Capricorn who tend to be outgoing. The fixed signs of Taurus, Leo, Scorpio and Aquarius tend to be rigid in their opinions. The mutable signs of Gemini, Virgo, Sagittarius and Pisces are flexible and adaptable.

Introduction

The third group refers to positivity/masculinity and negativity/femininity. The positive signs are Aries, Gemini, Leo, Libra, Sagittarius and Aquarius. These people tend to be extroverts. The negative/feminine signs are Taurus, Cancer, Virgo, Scorpio, Capricorn and Pisces and these people tend to be introverts. Do not be confused if you are a Cancer man as this does not mean that you lack masculinity any more than a woman with a masculine Sun sign lacks femininity, although Cancer is regarded as one of the most feminine signs.

Lastly the fourth group is known as the polarities. This indicates the special relationship a sign has with its polar opposite. Polar signs complement each other so that there is a special rapport and understanding between them. For example, as Cancer is the most maternal of signs, Capricorn, its polar opposite, is the most paternal Zodiac sign. Ruling planets – each sign is ruled by one of the planets, and each planet has a very similar energy to the sign it rules. For example, Cancer is ruled by the Moon, the Earth's satellite which controls the tides and, therefore, the emotions.

SUN SIGNS
WHAT ARE THEY?

The Sun is the star at the centre of our solar system which is composed of nine planets. The Earth is the third one out, at a distance of 93 million miles. The Sun is 109 times the size of the Earth and without it there would be no life. It is the most powerful of all the bodies in our solar system and exerts a gravitational pull upon all of us. It affects each of our personalities so strongly that a person who is born under a particular sign will continue to have those characteristics throughout their life. The Sun is the fuel of our solar system, just as the Sun is the fuel of your personality.

Your Sun sign, or sign of the Zodiac, depends on the month of the year that you were born in because the Earth travels around the Sun once in approximately 365 days and the Sun appears to travel through one of twelve constellations in the sky above.

Sun Signs – What are They?

Looking at your Sun sign should not be confused with studying the daily horoscopes that you will find in magazines or newspapers. In this book we are examining the effect that your Sun sign has on your personality rather than predictions. You were born between 21st June and 21st July which makes you a Cancer.

Some astrologers feel that Sun sign readings are too much of a generalisation, as if all butchers, bakers and candlestick makers were the same. However, the Sun, as I said earlier, is the most powerful body in our whole life which is reflected in the accuracy of Sun sign readings.

If you know someone's Sun sign you are most certainly much more informed about that person than not knowing it.

Your Sun sign personality is the personality that you present to people because it is what you cherish and it is what you are most proud of about yourself. To be more specific the placement of your Sun sign represents how you express your ego. In general a person's Sun sign will represent how they present themselves to the world during daylight hours and their Moon sign will represent how they present themselves as dusk arrives and their more intimate, hidden side comes out.

MOON SIGNS
WHAT ARE THEY?

The Moon is the Earth's satellite and is approximately 250,000 miles away. Although only small in diameter, 2,160 miles, the Moon exerts considerable gravitational influence on the Earth and is responsible for the tides. It orbits the Earth in approximately 28 days, known as the lunar cycle, and passes through each sign of the Zodiac every 2.5 days. In your birth chart it is considered almost as important as the Sun, but its influences are different. The Moon holds sway over your moods and emotional life. Whereas the Sun is your day, the Moon represents your night.

Your Moon sign represents how you deal with and express your tender, caring side and your emotional responses in general. It represents your instinctive, unconscious, primitive, habitual personality. How you express yourself is affected by your Moon sign. It represents

Moon Signs – What are They?

your basic emotional needs and how you interact with others. It represents your gut instinct and how you react to things when you are caught by surprise, particularly when you feel you are threatened. Another important area that the Moon controls is that of your domestic arena. Since it is the planet that rules Cancer, the Moon is seen as feminine, watery, negative and reflective.

Some people do have the same sign for the Sun and the Moon, so both their ego and emotions are ruled by the same sign. This will generally provide a pattern of consistency through many situations in your life.

Above: the Moon is seen as feminine, watery, negative and reflective.

CANCER

THE SUN SIGN

If you are a Cancer and if we met and I began to explain to you your personality through your horoscope, you would be more interested in your family's horoscopes than your own. Cancers love to mother more than anything else.

Cancer

21st June to 21st July

Positive Traits

Nurturing, caring, empathic, sensitive, intuitive, loving, sympathetic, imaginative, shrewd

Negative Traits

Moody, obstinate, oversensitive, over-emotional, sulky, suffocating

Traditional Associations

Zodiac Symbol: The Crab
Glyph: ♋
Ruling Planet: The Moon
Ruling House: The Fourth
Gender: Feminine and Negative
Polarity: Capricorn
Element: Water
Quality: Cardinal
Key Phrase: I Nurture
Body Area: The Breast and Chest
Colour: Amber
Metal: Silver
Gemstone: Moss Agate, Amber
Foods: Seafood, shellfish, milk, melon, tarragon
Flora: Waterlily, geranium, white rose, maple, rubber
Countries: Holland, Scotland, New Zealand, Algeria
Cities: Amsterdam, Manchester, New York, Istanbul, Venice, Tokyo, Wellington, Cadiz
Tarot Card: The Chariot
Deities: Diana and Selene
Activity: Home and Family

Cancer – the Sun Sign

Cancer is watery and ruled by the Earth's satellite, the Moon As a cardinal sign they are leaders in their own field. This is the most maternal and nurturing of the Zodiac signs, whether you are a man or a woman.

The fourth sign of the Zodiac, Cancer represents motherhood, mid-summer and domesticity. The sign for Cancer is the Crab and, accordingly, the Cancerian never goes anywhere directly. Crablike, they move sideways and, when thwarted, retreat into their shell. Their ruling sign is the Moon which controls the tides. Consequently, the

Above : Cancer represents motherhood, mid-summer and domesticity.

Cancer – the Sun Sign

moods of the Cancerian are tied in with the Moon and correlate to those same forces that cause the tides of the seas to flow in and out. Yet the Moon itself does not change, it just seems to. Likewise, the Cancerian remains the same person throughout all their highs and lows. Once it is known what phase the Crab is in at the time then it is possible to respond accordingly. One of the first things that is apparent with a Cancerian is their laughter. Crabs laugh at both their own jokes and those of others. No one has a better sense of humour and this aspect is all the more startling because it comes from a normally quiet and gentle personality. They do, however, secretly enjoy attention. They do not pursue fame with the passion of other signs, such as Leo, but they do not shrink from it either. Cancerians do hide in their shells from many things but appreciation is not one of them. Pessimism is never far away from the thoughts of the Crab and, although they have flights of imagination, they have an inner voice which keeps nagging them about the practicalities of life.

Crabs are very sensitive and can be deeply hurt by merely a harsh glance or a rough tone of voice. However, it is not easy to help when a Crab is down or hurt because they disappear into their shells. When they do snap your head off for some reason or

Cancer – the Sun Sign

another, it is not because they are angry with you necessarily; they are angry with life but they get over it very quickly. They do have to watch out for being passively aggressive and letting anger build up inside.

Cancerians have such strong imaginations and their moods are so intense that they can make all those around feel them, too. Their imagination seizes hold of joy, despair, horror, compassion, sorrow and ecstasy and retains each sensation in their amazing memories. Just like a camera they capture images and then reflect them. Every experience they have is engraved on their hearts and they never forget any of the lessons life has taught them.

They are particularly taken with history, almost worshipping the past, and they are usually extremely patriotic. Historical personages intrigue them as much as their own ancestors.

Above: one of the first things that is apparent with a Cancerian is their laughter. Crabs laugh at both their own jokes and those of others.

Cancer – the Sun Sign

Their deep sense of family tells them that we are all related and any historical figure may well be an ancestor. Their insatiable curiosity about the past is really about themselves. They are mental archaeologists, always digging for more interesting facts in history. They often collect antiques and ancient relics and have trouble throwing anything away as every object they have triggers a memory.

Cancerians rarely wear informal clothes. They enjoy dressing up as if they have already made their million. They exude an air of quality. When they do dress up, they dress traditionally with rich fabrics. Many Crabs are attracted to the theatre because it gives them a chance to dress in historical costumes. They also join historical re-enactment societies for the same reason. They like culture, but even the dreamiest Cancerians who spend their lives immersed in art and other cultural pursuits will be keeping an eye on the financial reward. It is rare to find a Cancerian living the bohemian life in an attic somewhere.

Above: Cancerians rarely wear informal clothes. They enjoy dressing up as if they have already made their million.

Cancer – the Sun Sign

Crabs are secretive people Although others will confide their secrets to the Crab, they rarely expose their own. They are compassionate and highly intuitive, but they guard their inner feelings carefully from others. They dislike discussing their personal lives unless the other person has been welcomed into their "family". They seldom judge; they simply gather, absorb and reflect like the Moon. Crabs transmit back the emotions of others like a mirror does but they do not reveal much about themselves.

They are highly possessive creatures by nature. This possessiveness has nothing to do with the value of an object. Each object or person that a Cancerian owns is their way of grounding themselves. Like the Crab they never go after what they want in an obvious manner. They will move backwards and sideways, weighing up what they desire before taking the plunge.

They behave in the same way when it comes to giving. Cancerians do have soft hearts and are always touched by other people's needs. They want to help everyone, but they wait first to see if someone else will help. They are very careful about giving away anything but if they do the gesture will be grand and generous. No one could ever accuse a Crab of being impulsive, though.

Cancer – the Sun Sign

Above all things, the Cancerian loves their home and they will devote most of their energy to it. It is the place where they play, love, dream and feel safe. They are never happy without a "hearth" to call their own. Crabs never feel secure no matter how much they own or how much love they get. They always need more. They are never secure enough to relax completely. They are always saving for a rainy day.

Second to the home, Cancerians love water, whether it is water-skiing or sailing, and many of them spend their leisure time on beaches or in boats. They feel the pull of the Moon on the tides calling them home. Their

Above: Cancerians love water, whether it is water-skiing or sailing, and many of them spend their leisure time on beaches or in their boats.

Cancer – the Sun Sign

moods are greatly affected by the phases of the Moon and around the time of the Full Moon Cancerians can become hyperactive or even manic.

Many of them have green fingers, producing beautiful gardens that they tend with love and care. They also attend to their saving accounts with the same devotion. Money clings to Cancer and they love the feel of it. They spend frugally. Food also represents security to a Cancer. They love to eat and they love to prepare delectable dishes for others. This is part of their deep nurturing instinct. The maternal instinct is just as strong in male Cancerians as in females. Crabs hover around their friends and loved ones protectively and naturally have a great love of children.

Above: many Cancerians have green fingers, producing beautiful gardens that they tend with love and care.

Cancer – the Sun Sign

YOUR BODY

Cancerians usually have fairly large skulls, an overhanging brow and high cheekbones. The brows themselves seem to knit together in a sort of permanent frown and the jawline is pronounced with teeth either prominent or irregular. Some of them put on weight easily, due to problems with water retention, but most of them have a strong bony structure, like the carapace of a crab. Their arms and legs may be extra long in proportion to the rest of the body. Their shoulders are broader than average and their hands and feet are either unusually tiny or unusually large. They seem to be top heavy and waddle slightly when they walk fast.

Cancerian women either have very large breasts or are absolutely flat-chested. This particular characteristic is quite marked. They all have very expressive features because many moods pass fleetingly across their faces in the course of a conversation. Their facial muscles therefore are used to working quite hard. Another Cancerian facial characteristic is that they have round faces, soft skin, circular eyes and a wide-grinning mouth, almost like the Man in the Moon.

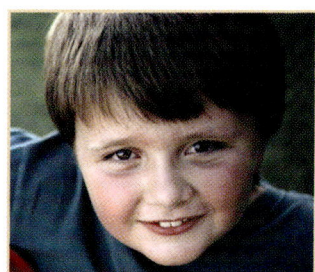

Above: Cancerians have round faces, soft skin, circular eyes and a wide-grinning mouth.

Cancer – the Sun Sign

YOUR POSSESSIONS

After Taurus, Crabs are the most possessive of all the signs. They want to own things to make themselves feel secure. It is not the intrinsic value of the things themselves that matters; it is the memories that these things hold for them. They are great hoarders and collectors of insignificant bric-a-brac. Their homes are often overflowing with bits and pieces they have collected on their travels. Wherever they go they tend to bring back souvenirs.

They are equally possessive about people. Once they have decided to accept someone as a friend and consequently into their extended family, they are there for life and they will mother everyone as if they were a child.

Cancerians are capable of communicating in many different ways, depending on what mood they are in and that of the recipient. They are able to observe human behaviour very carefully and communicate according to the prevailing atmosphere around them. They are never shallow or superficial. If they speak to someone who is angry then they reflect that. They also communicate a great deal through their facial expressions and never hide what they are feeling at that moment, although to pin them down on anything deeper is near impossible.

Cancer – the Sun Sign

YOUR HOME LIFE

For Cancerians, home and family is almost a religion and their mother is their goddess. Everything they do, think and feel pertains to home and family in one way or another. They spend most of their lives at home indoors. Many of them work in hotels for this very reason. They particularly enjoy restoring old property and improving everywhere they live. If they move somewhere new, they have to make their mark by changing everything to their requirements. They have a natural sense of Feng Shui as their homes have a harmony about them.

Crabs have large families and not only blood relatives as they will talk about their friends as family. A male friend will be referred to as a brother, a female friend as a sister. There is nothing they like better than gatherings of those closest to them, at their home. Christmas time is always their favourite time because they can do what they like most – that is feed and entertain their family in their own home. They may live in many different places throughout their lives but their home is always where their heart is. Indeed, they will often take their home with them by having a boat or a caravan. They always look forward to retiring to a cosy nest with a log fire, surrounded by all the many bits and pieces that they have gathered throughout their lives.

Cancer – the Sun Sign

Above: for Cancerians, Christmas time is always a favourite time because they can do what they like most – that is feed and entertain their family in their own home.

Cancer – the Sun Sign

YOUR CREATIVITY

Children are the second great love of Cancerians. Cancer is the sign of fertility and parenthood, particularly motherhood, and so they have an inborn need to create as many children as they possibly can and, if by any chance, they are unable to produce their own, they will adopt officially or unofficially as many others as they can. Many Cancerians are pet-mad and will regularly visit the local rescue centres looking for more "children" to adopt.

They are highly creative people in all senses. Sometimes they treat their gardens like their children or their pets. Cancer produces many great artists and they have a strong sense of colour and form. A Cancer's home will often have their own paintings on the walls. They also love to play music, particularly to entertain their friends and family. Crabs are very good at handicrafts and have very dextrous fingers. DIY and home furnishing are other ways they have of expressing themselves creatively.

Above: Cancer is the sign of fertility and parenthood, particularly motherhood, and so they have an inborn need to create as many children as they possibly can.

Cancer – the Sun Sign

YOUR HEALTH

Cancerians are ruled by their emotions. Their worries and their fears make them ill and their joys and their happiness make them well. Often when they say that they feel unwell what they really mean is that they are unhappy. If their security is threatened, either financially or romantically, they can fall into deep depression which in turn can trigger an illness or accident. Their over-active imagination can also turn a minor illness into a chronic one. When they are ill they do not respond to positive statements. They want sympathy for their plight but it is the last thing a Cancerian needs when they are ill, despite what they say. If they become melancholy through their fears and these are reinforced, they will take twice as long to recover.

Above: often when Cancerians say that they feel unwell what they really mean is that they are unhappy.

Cancer – the Sun Sign

Their most vulnerable areas are their chest and breast regions, kidneys, bladder and skin. They can be particularly prone to ulcers and digestive upsets, too. Dietary awareness can help all these problems.

What really keeps a Cancerian healthy is their sense of humour. If they do get a firm grip on happiness and in a crab-like way refuse to let go, they can cling to life with the same tenacity that they cling to the objects that they surround themselves with. No other sign is so prone to illness brought on by negative thinking but equally no other sign experiences such miraculous recoveries.

YOUR RELATIONSHIPS
Like all other aspects of the Cancerian their relationships go through phases. They can be gentle Moon maidens or "lunatics". They can laugh and cry at the same time. Crabs hate to be criticised and are deeply wounded by ridicule and rejection. They rarely make the first move in a relationship and when you make a move on them they will usually back away or move sideways to begin with. They are basically shy in one-to-one situations. Once a Cancerian has decided they want to have a relationship, either business or romance, they will begin to start the mothering process. They have quite deep feelings of inadequacy which they hide behind their hard exteriors.

Cancer – the Sun Sign

Above: Cancerians rarely make the first move in a relationship and are basically shy in one-to-one situations.

Cancer – the Sun Sign

Their rich humour is warm and affectionate but can sometimes turn into cynical wit and hypocritical laughter.

It is unfair to toy with the hearts of Cancerians because they will love, honour and obey their partner. When they nag they are doing so with sincere devotion. There is nothing shallow or superficial about the Crab's sentiments. When they commit to someone, they mean it, forever.

They may not be vivacious or forthcoming with flattery but they are always charming. They reserve showing their emotions only to the people closest to them. The slightest, unintentional remark mark can wound them deeply. It is also hard to know when they are vulnerable. Female Cancerians cry a lot and the males, when they do cry, will always do so alone.

Crabs can be flirtatious and fickle but, when they find the right person, they are sensitive and loyal. The "right person" is likely to be a parental figure rather than a wild party animal.

Above: when Cancerians find the right person they are sensitive and loyal. The "right person" is likely to be a parental figure rather than a wild party animal.

Cancer – the Sun Sign

YOUR RESOURCES

Cancerians treasure and guard the things they own with great jealousy and find it difficult to share their resources. They will, of course, share their emotions. They save as much money as they possibly can and will often live below their means in order to save up for a rainy day. When they invest they think about it very carefully and only put their finances into solid, safe investments. They excel at trading and are masters at figuring out what people want and then supplying it at a substantial profit.

Above: Cancerians save as much money as they possibly can and will often live below their means in order to save up for a rainy day.

Cancer – the Sun Sign

YOUR EDUCATION

The lure of cash entices many Cancerians away from their education and many of them become self-made entrepreneurs. If they do go to university, you can be sure that they will work part-time and save the money that they earn or they will choose to go later on in life, after they have made their money.

Above: Cancerians may leave their education early in order to pursue a paying job but may return to their education later in life.

Cancer – the Sun Sign

YOUR CAREER AND AMBITIONS

Cancerians are serious and hard-working people. Whatever career that they decide upon they will work unceasingly towards success, and success for them means money. Their attitude is that the harder they work, the more money they will make. They also expect the whole world to have the same philosophy. Some of the most successful people in commerce are Crabs.

Those who have inherited wealth and position will still continue to build up more and more. They have insatiable appetites for cash. For them charity begins at home. They are most successful in careers such as merchandising, catering, interior design and decorating, museums, property, gardening, banking and shipping.

Above: Cancerians may find a successful career in catering.

Cancer – the Sun Sign

YOUR FRIENDS

Cancerians do not have friends, they have family. They like to be the centre of attention amongst their friends, in the same way that a mother is in a family. They need to be needed by their friends; they exemplify the saying "a friend in need is a friend indeed". They accumulate people and will protect them with great tenacity should a situation arise. However, anyone who falls out with them will soon know it as they can be emotionally manipulative as well vindictive. Crabs tend to cut off those who offend them, not only from themselves but from the entire "family" group.

They hope to have a large family, whatever form that may take, and lots of money in order to create a secure and comfortable home. A Crab's worst fear is losing their security, both financial and domestic.

Cancer – the Sun Sign

Above: Cancerians like to be the centre of attention amongst their friends, in the same way that a mother is in a family.

THE 12
MOON SIGNS

To find out your Moon sign either consult a professional astrologer or go to my website www.jamespetulengro.co.uk for a free birth chart.

ARIES

An Aries Moon means that you are extremely assertive in your nature on a subconscious level. Through the influence of Mars, life to you is one big adventure, with your ego ruling your feelings. You may come across as pushy because of your continual drive for success and your high self-motivation. You are very open to new ideas and concepts and can make quick decisions based on your instincts. It is rare that you use reasoning skills, preferring instead to leap into action. You often lose your temper over the smallest thing without a thought for the consequences. What you are thinking gets said as your mind is always active and

The 12 Moon Signs

your emotions explode out of you, often before you have thought things through.

You are a bit of a rogue at times, with a "joie de vivre" which attracts many people to you. You are emotionally independent and will develop detachment from the people around you except perhaps from your immediate loved ones whom you will put on a pedestal. You feel with your ego.

Advice is something that you rarely take, preferring instead to rely on your own instincts. If someone gives you advice when it is not asked for, you can fly off the handle very quickly. The Moon in Aries can indicate a sense of

insecurity behind your independent and assertive exterior. You love challenges, particularly from a worthy opponent but react emotionally when you lose. You rarely compromise, particularly when it comes to your feelings. However, when it comes to romance, someone who can stand up to you will earn your respect.

At home you have an enthusiasm for DIY, but you need to be in control of both the design and the work. This can often lead to domestic disputes.

The 12 Moon Signs

TAURUS

A Taurus Moon means that you place great emphasis on material possessions. Your emotions are focused on getting the best that life has to offer. In terms of comfort, you cannot go without all of life's luxuries. You enjoy making your home environment beautiful and tasteful. You have a great love of collecting things, including people, and you can be extremely possessive about your friends and lovers. Emotionally you are very down-to-earth and practical and spend your time working to achieve your material desires in order to lead the good life that you feel you deserve. You have a natural business sense and can be very successful in the world of finance. The Moon is very stable in this sign as your emotional responses are slow but well thought out.

The 12 Moon Signs

As a friend you are good-natured, loyal and easygoing. You rarely lose your temper but, when you do, you can be very formidable. You would rather love than fight and can be very surprised at other people's rages. Small grievances rarely bother you. You have strong physical appetites and a deep emotional need to gratify them. You are very determined but sometimes stubborn and self-indulgent, particularly for the good things in life.

You are a sensual and affectionate lover, and highly sexed, but you have a tendency to be over-possessive as you have a strong sense of ownership with both things and people. Your voice is pleasantly harmonious to others and you may well love singing and dancing and the arts in general as Taurus is ruled by Venus, goddess of beauty.

You are generally very conservative in your outlook and once you have decided what is true about life, you will stick to it and find change of any kind difficult. You must avoid becoming too narrow-minded in your opinions.

The 12 Moon Signs

GEMINI

A Gemini Moon makes you witty and articulate with a tendency to feel with your mind. You are adaptable in your ideas and very attracted to mental stimulation. You enjoy socialising and the sign of the twins indicates a happy and easy-going personality. Your trademark is observation and you have a great gift for verbalising all of your ideas. You are friendly and gregarious and will have many friends, lovers and acquaintances. You truly love people of all kinds and being ruled by Mercury, the messenger god, communication is your whole life. You are never at a loss for words but sometimes you can get carried away and end up arguing with yourself, both in your own mind and in conversations and debates. This sometimes confuses people as to what you really believe, as you can change your mind as quickly as you can change your clothes. In fact, you are likely to do both several times during a day.

The 12 Moon Signs

Your moods can be very changeable, up one moment and down the next, and you tend to be nervous in your movements. Some people may think you are shallow, but actually you are torn apart by constantly changing feelings.

Your restless nature is always searching for new stimuli. Although you may not do too well academically you are a life-long student of knowledge itself and, like a butterfly, your mind will flit from subject to subject taking sustenance from each.

You have a great sense of humour and will be very entertaining at parties, although sometimes you can seem too cynical for some people and you can hurt people with cutting remarks which you will forget as quickly as you said them.

You are romantically inclined but in an intellectual way. You are fascinated more by the mind of your lovers than by their bodies. You are not the most faithful of the signs as you are always looking for something or someone better around the next corner. You are not the domestic type as you are moving around too much to settle down, until perhaps much later in life. You do not like to be tied down to one person or one place; freedom is important to you and you hate being restricted by emotional attachments.

The 12 Moon Signs

CANCER

A Cancer Moon is highly sensitive due to the fact that it is ruled by the Moon. Therefore, you can be moody and broody and your moods will fluctuate through the month, as the Moon changes from New to Full.

You are highly maternal and will mother all your friends and family if they will let you. You need to be careful not to smother them. You also have a deep and powerful capacity to memorise every experience and to re-experience it in great detail whenever you want. You also have a strong intuition and an almost psychic ability to tune in to other people's thoughts and emotions and to the atmosphere of places. You should trust in your gut feelings and hunches but because you are, by nature, suspicious and distrusting you must be careful that this does not turn into paranoia. Whatever you feel, always remember that the Moon is affecting it. You go through cycles of feeling more than

The 12 Moon Signs

any other sign. You must be careful not to mistake your feelings for the feelings of the people around you that you are picking up on.

You are gentle, peaceful and romantic, and appreciative of all that is feminine in life. You have a great love of home and family which you will protect with your life. Of all the signs you are the greatest homemaker. Your domestic life needs to be safe and secure as this is the shell into which the crab that you are will retreat when disturbed. Some people only see your hard outer shell and forget that inside you are soft and kind.

You are particularly interested in history and your ancestors and Cancer Moons love their country. You need to feel that you are in control of the whole world and can become withdrawn and ill when you lose control of any part of it. Change is not something that you relish.

Above: you have a great love of home and family which you will protect with your life.

The 12 Moon Signs

LEO

Leo Moons have a sunny disposition and a desire to lead in all walks of life. You are generally confident, cheerful and optimistic. Emotionally you are happy-go-lucky and hedonistic. You are self-sufficient and self-reliant, and deeply emotionally involved in all undertakings. You love display and pageants, especially if you are personally involved in them. This may lead you to being involved in drama, whether on the stage or in the home. You feel that you can do anything that you want and your creative ability feels as though it has no bounds. You may appear to others to be haughty and somewhat spoilt. This is because you have a tendency to think of yourself as royalty and the rest of humanity as your subjects. You have a need to be admired and even applauded and you are constantly seeking appreciation and attention. You have a natural creative flair in the home with a gift for interior design, and

The 12 Moon Signs

your surroundings will always be flamboyant and probably expensive. You think of your home as your palace and, in seeking to impress others, you may well overspend at times. You are a social climber and demand respect from all those around you. You are straightforward and usually dignified, enabling you to gain responsibility and status. Nothing hurts you more than when you feel unappreciated and your pride has been stepped upon. You have a natural nobility but you can be egocentric and even pompous. It is very difficult for you to back down or accept any sort of compromise – after all you are the Ruler.

You are a loving and devoted parent and will cosset and play with your children with great affection and warmth. You love giving and have a great sense of charity towards those worse off than you. You are highly emotional with a strong drive for power and prominence.

Above: you are a loving and devoted parent and will cosset and play with your children with great affection and warmth.

The 12 Moon Signs

VIRGO

Virgo Moons are reserved, analytical and critical. You may seem unemotional to others as it is difficult for you to express what you feel. Consequently, you can come across as cold and detached and can sometimes seem prudish and stuffy, when in fact you are highly emotional and easily hurt.

You may have a deep-seated inferiority complex which may lead you to prove yourself through your intellectual superiority. You always consider the practical application of study rather than just learning for its own sake.

You are generally shy and so you respond well to encouragement and appreciation, although you rarely give this to others. You are your own worst enemy and assume that because you are over-critical of yourself that others do the same.. You have very little in the way of self-esteem. You may feel that people don't like you, for this is a placement that shows

The 12 Moon Signs

much lack of self-esteem, thus you tend to be emotionally reserved. Your talents lie in expressing your feelings through writing and poetry as your Moon is ruled by Mercury, the messenger god. Consequently you will be ruled by your mind rather than by your heart and you will have trouble understanding highly emotional and passionate people. Your reactions often seem detached and rather cold. Self-analysis may occupy a lot of your thoughts and in fact psychoanalysis and psychiatry would be good careers for you.

You are too introverted to have a strong sex drive and you will be shy about the physical act and have difficulty in accepting its undignified side. Within a relationship you will attempt to make yourself indispensable to your partner, thereby securing your love, and you respond well to responsibility. In the home you are particularly concerned with hygiene, health and diet and will be constantly involved in tidying up and cleaning.

Virgo Moon is earthy so you are practical and have a definite sense of the realities of life. You are at your best when you are taking care of someone who is in need of you. You can be temperamental and argumentative, but you have a shrewd business sense and pay meticulous attention to detail.

The 12 Moon Signs

LIBRA

Libra Moons are gentle and tolerant, and have a great sense of beauty and justice. You are, above all things, dependent upon your personal relationships. The symbol of Libra, the scales, signifies balance and symmetry in all things. You are diplomatic, broad-minded, social and make pleasant company. You dislike disorder and spend a great deal of your time organising your busy social life. You are even-tempered, well-mannered and graceful in movement. As you are ruled by Venus, art and beauty are paramount in your life, as is your search for the perfect partner. You cannot bear coarseness or vulgarity and will seek relationships with cultured and educated people. You are highly adaptable and dislike disputes, conflicts and disorder. Your gentle nature will bring you many friends, although, because of your tendency to weigh things in the balance, you may never be sure of how you feel about people. You can find it hard to make up your mind quickly and will spend a great deal of time considering the various possibilities and options open to you in all areas of your life.

The 12 Moon Signs

Your home, which is very important to you, will be harmonious and tranquil and full of beautiful objects. You are particularly attracted towards the arts and may make a career in this direction. Anything that you can make more beautiful will be given a makeover, including people.

You enjoy the company of people and do not like to spend much time alone. You need to be liked and your emotional well-being depends on being appreciated for the beautiful person that you really are, for you truly are a thoughtful and good-natured person who will go out of their way to be kind to others. At many times in your life you will seem to be in crisis and have difficulty in making decisions because you are capable of seeing both sides equally. As often as not your decision will be based on the toss of a coin. You can sometimes be too willing to compromise and frequently allow others to take advantage of you in the name of peace and because it is easier to let other people make decisions. For your partner you can be self-sacrificing and happy to fulfil his or her needs before your own.

A solid, steady relationship is your preference. You love to receive small gifts and you are a romantic at heart. You do your best to spread beauty and harmony wherever you can.

The 12 Moon Signs

SCORPIO

Scorpio Moons are the most passionate and secretive of all the signs. You are highly sensitive and have an uncanny memory which leads you to remember both pleasant and unpleasant memories which can sometimes leave deep psychic scars. You enjoy life to the full and have an innate understanding that through suffering character is formed. You are the most sexual of all signs, but you combine your sexuality with deep spirituality.

Pluto, the ruler of the underworld can lead you into the depths of your unconscious where you may find disturbing feelings but, having entered into your underworld, you return strangely refreshed and born anew. You have a great capacity for regeneration and will 'die' many times in your lifetime. Change is what you thrive on. You need to learn to come to terms with your deep emotions as other signs are not as emotionally intense as you. You may find that

The 12 Moon Signs

you see other people as shallow. Your real nature is not openly apparent to others as, until you get to know somebody deeply, you tend to hide your true feelings but once you love, you love passionately and the object of your affection can take over your whole existence. This can also be so for your children as you will bestow an all-consuming love upon them. You are a good homemaker, provided that you get your own way in it but you prefer the company of your immediate family rather than entertaining all and sundry.

In all your relationships you are extremely possessive and jealous and can even become violent when your passions are thwarted. No-one says "no" to a Scorpio Moon. You can be domineering and will often use your sexual favours to get what you want. You have a problem with judging people too quickly and, if they make a mistake, you rarely give them a second chance. You react to emotional situations in an abrupt and impulsive way. You can also be vindictive, spiteful and vengeful when wronged and are easily hurt. You are very determined in achieving your ambitions and thrive on new challenges. You are an extremist by nature and never pursue anything light-heartedly; even when a situation becomes detrimental you insist on seeing it through to the end.

The 12 Moon Signs

SAGITTARIUS

A Sagittarius Moon indicates feelings of restlessness and requires a great deal of physical activity in order to disperse pent-up emotion. You need your freedom to wander where and when you will. You are happy-go-lucky, enthusiastic and highly optimistic and at your best when you are mobile. Because of your eternal optimism you can be socially naïve and blissfully unaware of social differences. This can sometimes make you socially inept because you tend to see all people as equals. You have high ideals and meet people on your own terms by melting and merging into relationships with them like a friendly puppy does. You are generally good-natured, fun loving and jovial like Jupiter that rules this sign. You always know who you are and where you are heading, but

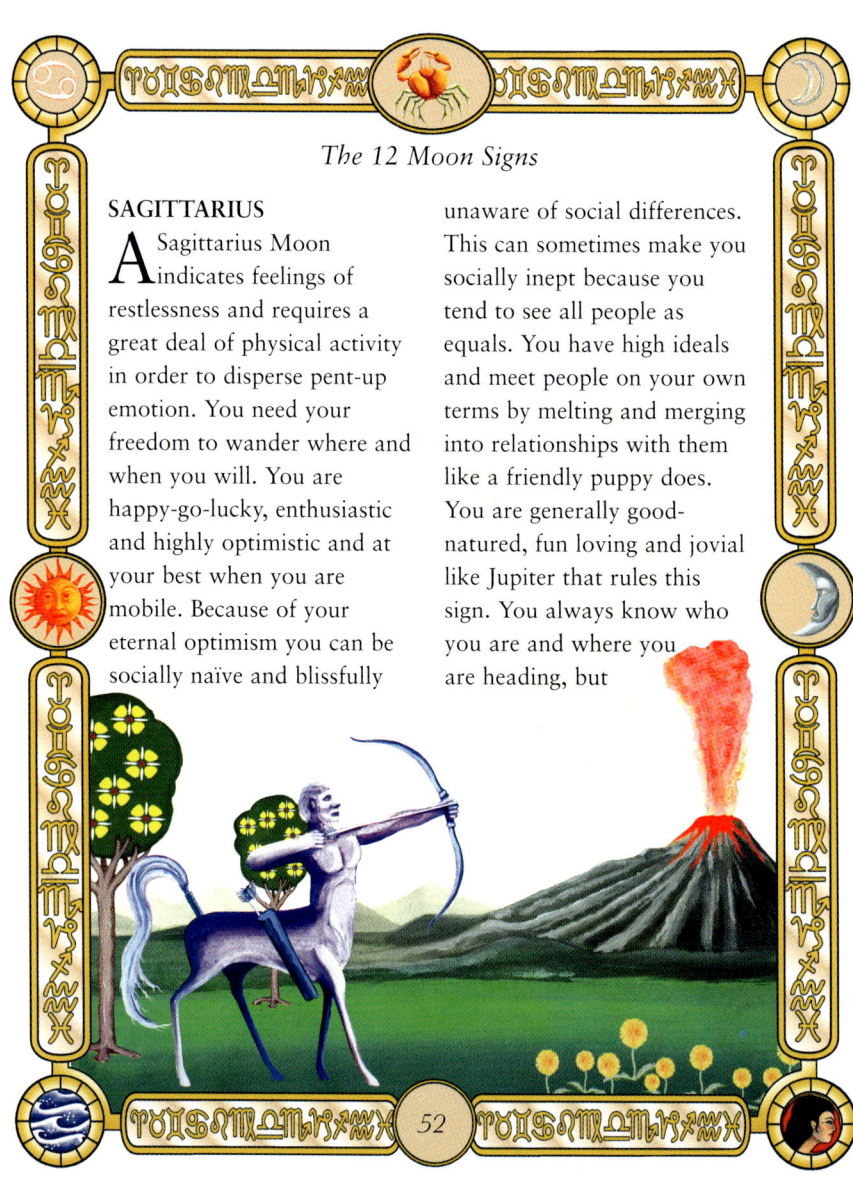

The 12 Moon Signs

adaptable enough to change direction when it feels that you will learn more.

Learning is very important to you, although you have a tendency not to learn from your mistakes. The learning that you are interested in is the knowledge of all things, particularly the mysteries of the universe. You make a fine teacher or spiritual adviser.

Your home may not be tidy, but it is filled with objects that you have gathered on your travels. You will be very enthusiastic in teaching your children everything they want to know and encouraging them to expand their knowledge whenever you can, being more of a friend than a parent.

It is important to you that your partners are also your friends as well as your lovers. You display your affections openly and need a partner who will play, socialise and travel places with you without making too many demands. Being free and without restraints is one of your deepest needs.

Sporting activities will help keep your weight down as you have a predisposition to overindulge in eating and drinking.

You are prone to many changes in your life, particularly to changes of residence or career which you need to fulfil your restless nature.

The 12 Moon Signs

CAPRICORN

Capricorn Moons want to be recognised as important and powerful people because they were raised that way. You were likely to have had a strong parental influence. You are determined, steadfast and reliable. You are geared up to lead and have a strong sense of politics. You are the most ambitious of all the signs and the most likely to succeed in your emotional arena.

You seek power and are continually "climbing mountains". Once you have reached the top of your particular mountain it is guaranteed that you will notice a higher one in the distance and off you will go again. Expressing your emotions can sometimes be difficult and some people may see you as unfeeling but you are not. Your emotions are centred on your career and it is hard for you to relax and surrender to the simple pleasures of life. You are the parent of the Zodiac

The 12 Moon Signs

because you are ruled by Saturn, the god of time. Because of this, you are likely to seem old when you are young and young when you are old. Some Moon in Capricorns have a Peter-Pan complex but only inside; on the outside they appear to be wise beyond their years. Whatever your goals are you will strive to achieve them, stubbornly and persistently. You are a very hard worker and will take on goals that would frighten other signs.

You are conservative in your emotions, not in a political sense, but in a true sense of conservation. This is your way – not to create new things but to improve upon and conserve what has come before you. If you are thwarted in your goals, you can become despondent and moody and begin to look at the negative side of things. You need to develop a more optimistic approach to life. Capricorn Moons can be shy but have a very clever sense of humour and can lead people to do what they want with this humour.

Your home life, like your career, will be ambitious. You will want to live in the best house in the best part of town. A Capricorn Moon loves renovating old property and your taste is normally classical. A lot of Capricorn Moons work from home due to their tendency to be shy and self-conscious about their

The 12 Moon Signs

feelings which they would really rather not have. With your children you are likely to be a disciplinarian and have as much ambition for them as you have for yourself. Sometimes you can be disappointed because they don't have the same drive, and it can be hard for you to show your deep feelings of affection towards them. You may aspire to being a member of the aristocracy and you are most certainly a social climber, although you would prefer to entertain at home than to go to parties. It is rare to find a Capricorn Moon who leaves the world poorer than he or she entered it. You are the most reserved of signs, particularly in the way you communicate and interact with others. Your driving ambitions are usually successful but sometimes at the cost of romantic life.

Security and stability are very important to you as are financial gain and establishing yourself as a community leader. You are a traditionalist in life and have solid values and morals.

The 12 Moon Signs

AQUARIUS

Aquarius Moons produce the most modern and progressive people of all the signs. However, you can sometimes be erratic in some of the ideals you hold. You are unusual and unpredictable, with a broad imagination. You are most likely to engage in many kinds of group activities and have a wide range of friends from all walks of life. You have a capacity to see inside people and not be taken in by appearances. For you a beggar may be an angel in disguise.

You have a very creative imagination and your many friends will value your input into their lives. Sometimes your high ideals can get in the way of practicality and common sense. You have a quality that puts you ahead of your time and some people may see you as downright eccentric. You are attracted to all things that are modern and innovative as you are ruled by Uranus, the god of change. You love the sciences and would dearly love to invent something to improve the lot of humanity.

The 12 Moon Signs

In your relationships you demand a great deal of freedom and prefer partners who will treat you equally, regardless of your gender. You can at times seem impersonal in your personal relationships because you have the ability to love many people and sometimes find it difficult to express your emotions to your loved ones. It does not mean to say that you don't love them, it's just that you expect them to understand that you love everybody.

Your home life will be unusual and possibly bohemian in nature, possibly with many changes of residence, not necessarily all of the bricks and mortar variety. You will be interested in aromatherapy and natural remedies and you may surround yourself with electronic gadgets. As a parent you will be very liberal with your children, hoping that they will believe in your high ideals.

You are, above all things, a humanitarian. You abhor human suffering and do all you can to alleviate it.

The 12 Moon Signs

PISCES

A Moon in Pisces means that you have a great understanding of what it is to be human, albeit in a somewhat dreamy sense. You are gifted with great sensitivity and perception, allowing you to have great compassion and consideration for other people. This Moon means you have great empathy towards others in a psychic way and you often experience their emotions.

Since Neptune, the god of the sea rules your Moon, you need to ensure that you are not flooded by people's moods and desires psychically. Therefore you should meditate and reflect on your own feelings in solitude. Life to you is permanently rose-tinted, no matter how harsh the reality. Everyone's "little faults" are ignored, no matter how big.

At times, though, your optimism and unselfishness can leave you open to others taking advantage of your passive nature. Your misplaced trust means that you often end up hurt and feeling sorry for yourself. Rather than blame the other person, you tend to turn in on yourself, again resulting in melancholy.

The 12 Moon Signs

You will spend a great deal of your time searching for answers to life's great questions and will read a great many books on a wide variety of subjects. At times you will seek a more spiritual way of life. You are surprisingly ambitious and, because of your gift of creative visualisation, you can achieve your goals.

However, you do not have the competitive drive of other signs and so can lack self-confidence.

The 12 Moon Signs

Trust is something that you do not give freely. When you are entirely comfortable with someone you can then be surprisingly bossy as this is your way of showing that you trust them. In marriage you are so supportive that you are in danger of becoming a martyr. You need love and approval and, although you can live alone, you prefer to give and receive love.

Sometimes you can be so shy and repressed that you do not find the love you require and instead retreat into yourself. As a parent you empathise with your children but prefer those that can actively respond rather than young babies.

You are incredibly romantic and love all the little things which make up a relationship. Sex is something you enjoy as it combines all your favourite feelings and sensations.

Your home is your haven, a place where you can withdraw from the hustle and bustle of everyday life. However, you will also have many friends and visitors coming and going, particularly as you rarely lock your doors. People are drawn to you because they know that you are a good shoulder to cry on and will assist as much as possible with their personal problems. You need to ensure, however, that you do not sacrifice yourself for others too much.

CANCER SUN
AND THE 12 MOON SIGN COMBINATIONS

When you calculate a birth chart you will discover that the Moon as well as the planets will sometimes be in different signs of the Zodiac. The whole chart gives the whole picture of the personality, but the Sun and the Moon have the most powerful effect upon us. When you combine the Sun sign and the Moon sign you are combining different parts of the Zodiac. Some signs work well together and some signs don't, in the same way that two Sun signs may live in eternal conflict where others live in harmony; so it is with the Sun and Moon in your chart. What follows is an explanation of the combinations between your Cancer Sun and various other moons that may appear in your birth chart.

CANCER SUN WITH ARIES MOON

This combination of your reflective Sun sign with a fiery Moon sign produces a sensitive personality with sparky mental processes and an astounding memory. Although you believe in your own abilities greatly and approach life in a very determined fashion, you are not egotistical. You show a

Cancer Sun and the 12 Moon Sign Combinations

great deal of sensitivity to the feelings of others. You are very straightforward with your own feelings and treat others as you expect to be treated yourself. However, if you are aroused or offended your emotions show quickly as they are always close to the surface. You respond quickly and abruptly but your temper soon cools down and returns to normal after the initial explosion.

You care deeply about people but can be impatient with them at times. You say things impulsively without having first thought them through, even though you mean well. You are quick to dismiss the opinions of your friends and colleagues, but will do your utmost to defend them if they are under attack from elsewhere. Although you enjoy the comforts of a good home, your Aries Moon means that you get bored if you spend too much time there and you need to find an arena where you can experience some conflict.

You are a shrewd business person and enjoy competition in your career, although ideas and people appeal to you more than the financial side.

Mars and the Moon, the two ruling forces, could not be more different and hence the unusual paradoxes found in this combination.

Cancer Sun and the 12 Moon Sign Combinations

CANCER SUN WITH TAURUS MOON

The combination of your watery Sun and your earthy Moon sign produces a very nurturing and sensitive individual who shows they care through physical means. You are well-liked and always willing to give a supportive hug or cuddle to any friend who needs one. You charm people with your gracious and loving nature and you are renowned for your kindness. Although you are very honest and frank in your opinions, you express them in a very pleasant and diplomatic manner.

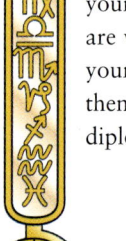

You are very determined and purposeful in all your undertakings but do so in a very modest and kind-hearted fashion, although you are inclined to laziness at times. Overall, you have a good head for business and are extremely adept at handling people. You can also do very well in accumulating wealth and making sound financial investments as silver seems to flow in your direction. Although you are reluctant to part with your money, you do appreciate and enjoy life's little luxuries and often splash out on indulgences, especially in the artistic or musical fields.

Cancer Sun and the 12 Moon Sign Combinations

Your family and your home are of the utmost importance to you and you guard them fiercely. Although you have many friends, you find very close, personal relationships difficult to make as you do not find it easy to relate to people who do not think and feel the same way as you. You are very shrewd about who you let in to your innermost secrets and feelings. However, once you find that special someone who is equally considerate then you are loyal and sincere.

Above: once you find that special someone who is equally considerate then you are loyal and sincere.

Cancer Sun and the 12 Moon Sign Combinations

CANCER SUN WITH GEMINI MOON

The combination of your cardinal Sun sign and your mutable Moon sign produces an extremely sensitive and intuitive personality with a fast-working mind. Your caring nature means you are eager to accommodate the needs of others and you adapt accordingly. Although your flexibility is a strength, it can sometimes leave you open to being hurt as you place your trust all too easily. You have a tendency to hide in your shell if you get too badly hurt.

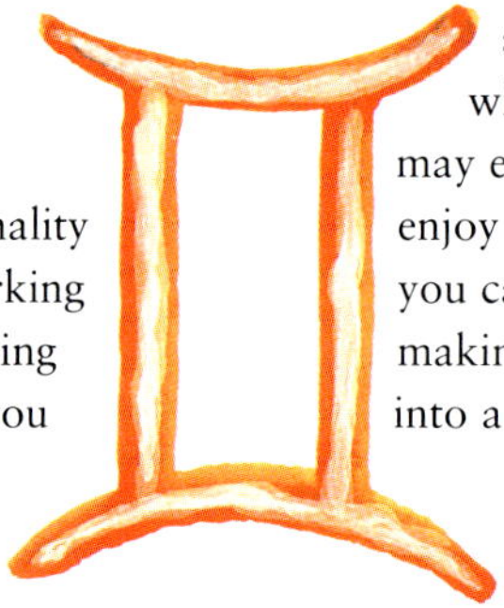

You enjoy socialising and love to be part of a group. If you are left out of any event then you are extremely hurt.

Sporting events are something that people with this combination may excel in. You also enjoy travelling, as long as you can be certain of making anywhere you stay into a home from home.

You may appear slow on the surface but underneath is a lightning-quick mind. You are very good at speaking, particularly in public. You can be very successful in the world of business or politics, albeit somewhat indecisive at times due to the duality of Gemini.

Cancer Sun and the 12 Moon Sign Combinations

Your staying power at a task can also be a problem as you often experience self-doubt if something does not go your way on the first attempt. This is something else that can cause you to give up and retreat into your shell.

CANCER SUN WITH CANCER MOON

You were born at the time of the New Moon and the double combination of Cancer Sun and Cancer Moon signs amplifies the natural traits of the sign. This is the most sensitive of all the combinations, and you are truly a feeling person above all things. You are quite reserved and may sometimes seem aloof. You rarely make the first move in relationships. It is difficult for you to understand that other people have their own problems and because of this you may feel ignored or left out. It is difficult for you to come out

Above: if you are left out of any event then you are extremely hurt.

Cancer Sun and the 12 Moon Sign Combinations

of your shell to socialise with people. It is not that you are self-centred but you sometimes give that impression.

Your shell or your home is where you are happiest as you feel safe there away from the constantly changing world around you. Indeed you experience emotional overload unless you are on your own.

Because of your hypersensitivity towards others, you can sometimes be very suspicious of people and quite touchy, as if someone is going to upset you at any time. It takes a long time for someone to win your confidence. Although you are not likely to marry early – and your introverted nature makes it hard for you to establish a relationship – when you do, you become extremely domestic and make an over-protective parent.

If you can come out from your protective carapace, you are an extremely warm and genial person with a great sense of humour. You are also an old-fashioned romantic at heart. You make an excellent diplomat as you are not confrontational in your approach. You are kind-hearted and highly aware of the needs of others. You are strongly attached to the past and tradition and would make an excellent historian or archaeologist.

Cancer Sun and the 12 Moon Sign Combinations

CANCER SUN WITH LEO MOON

The combination of your Sun and Moon sign means you are ruled by both the Sun and the Moon. This makes you a lot more extroverted than other Cancerians. You have a positive and confident personality with a great deal of pride, dignity and self-esteem. Others find you open-hearted, outgoing and friendly. You always make a good first impression because you care a great deal about what others think of you. This leads to you getting a great deal of support and respect from the people you come into contact with.

It is important to you that you are popular and you can sometimes go out of your way to get the attention and respect that you desire. Although you have this warm, sunny personality, you keep most people at a distance and only get close to people that you have tested in loyalty. You tolerate people's shortcomings because you feel that you are in control of most circumstances that you find yourself in. In unexpected situations you manage to do the right thing at the right time. You dislike being around sloppy and untidy people because in yourself you are always neat and organised. You may take

Cancer Sun and the 12 Moon Sign Combinations

yourself too seriously at times and perhaps appear a little pompous and self-righteous. You have a talent for getting your own way by making your opponents feel that they are the winners and that you are the one making compromises.

Sometimes your high standards can lead you to cut off your nose to spite your face. For all your outer confidence you are still emotionally vulnerable inside, although you still have a hard core of determination which always gets you your own way.

CANCER SUN WITH VIRGO MOON

The combination of your watery Sun sign and your mercurial Moon sign strengthens many of the traits that the two signs have in common. This makes you conventional, cautious and unpretentious in your approach to life. You combine the emotional sensitivity of the Moon with the discrimination and practical virtues of the earthy Virgo. You have the ability to use your reason and your emotions to stay controlled in all situations. Your caring attitude makes you attractive to many people.

Cancer Sun and the 12 Moon Sign Combinations

You are able to manage your affairs with a cool and calm detachment, giving the impression that you are sure of yourself. You need time to reflect on situations until you make your decisions and then you make the right choice.

You have an astounding memory and your confidence increases as you mature. This is because you absorb knowledge and master details as you go through life. You have a fine, rational and analytical mind. However, your hunches can often miss the mark, particularly when you are judging other people as you are overly suspicious of people's motives. You are especially skilled at sensing other people's needs. Because you handle authority well and respect rules, laws and traditions, you have a natural inclination to serve the needs of the community in some way. The medical profession would be particularly suited to your personality.

Above: the medical profession would be particularly suited to your personality.

Cancer Sun and the 12 Moon Sign Combinations

CANCER SUN WITH LIBRA MOON

The combination of your watery Sun and airy Moon indicates a personality full of contradictions. Your lunar side will want to hide and wallow in emotion whereas your Venusian side wants you to remain detached and analytical, creating a constant pull between objectivity and emotion. What you are looking for most is companionship but it is hard for you to give much of yourself because of your over-sensitive and introverted nature. However, your natural charm makes people respond to you in a relaxed way. You are socially adept but better in large gatherings than on a more intimate basis. You are a born romantic and enjoy the fact that people fall in love with you easily. You like the company of lots of people, particularly if they flirt with you, although you may have difficulty in responding in kind.

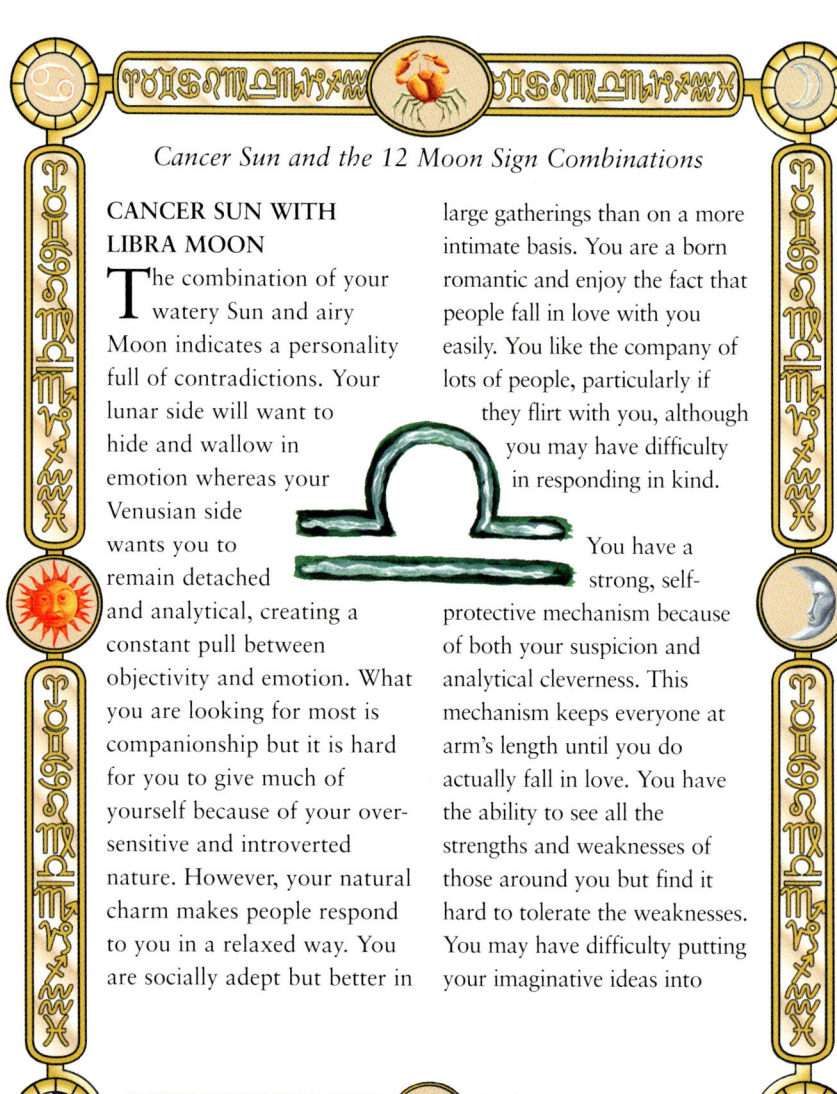

You have a strong, self-protective mechanism because of both your suspicion and analytical cleverness. This mechanism keeps everyone at arm's length until you do actually fall in love. You have the ability to see all the strengths and weaknesses of those around you but find it hard to tolerate the weaknesses. You may have difficulty putting your imaginative ideas into

Cancer Sun and the 12 Moon Sign Combinations

CANCER SUN WITH SCORPIO MOON

This double watery combination of your Sun and Moon sign produces a personality like a wild and stormy sea. You are temperamental and have great power but your emotions are so close to the surface and so quickly triggered that it takes a great deal of patience for people to reach you. You are intense and highly dramatic. You have a magnetic appeal and a commanding persona. Many people are drawn to you, not because you are popular but impelling. If you can keep your feelings under control, there is no limit to what you practice but you do have a talent for business. You could well be drawn into the artistic field, particularly the spheres of music or art. You also have a need to spend time by water in order to recharge your batteries.

Above: you could well be drawn into the artistic field, particularly the spheres of music or art.

Cancer Sun and the 12 Moon Sign Combinations

can accomplish. On the other hand, when you allow your temper to have full rein, you can be equally destructive. You have a talent for dedication and devotion to whatever you focus upon.

Although you may appear to be cruel at times, it is only a quick reaction because you are not intentionally unkind or mean. You are deeply protective of your family and feel that you would die for them. You have great worldly ambition but mostly for fortune rather than fame and you enjoy money. You are deeply romantic and lavish in your affections but your deeply jealous nature can loosen your temper at times. You also find it hard to allow people too close. You have a defensive side to your nature, even when you do not need to be so, and you are constantly looking out for potentially threatening situations. You must try to keep a positive outlook on life and avoid being too pessimistic.

Above: you are deeply protective of your family and feel that you would die for them.

Cancer Sun and the 12 Moon Sign Combinations

CANCER SUN WITH SAGITTARIUS MOON

This combination of your fixed Sun with a mutable Moon sign makes for a much more social and progressive kind of Cancerian. You have the ability to relate to ideals but on a very real and practical basis. You inspire confidence in others, but you demand absolute openness and honesty from them. You come across as loveable. When you do detect falsity and insincerity in people your sensitive and defensive side quickly puts up barriers. You hate petty jealousies, gossip and spiteful behaviour. You have your own set of rules and high standards and probably have a role model or philosophy that is your inspiration.

Although you are extremely polite and tactful, you have no difficulty being firm and assertive. You communicate in a frank and open way and are outspoken on all the issues that you believe in. Although you have high ideals, you may ask for more than is possible to obtain on occasion.

In many ways you are a free spirit. A career at sea would suit you well as you enjoy being on the water and seeing places.

Cancer Sun and the 12 Moon Sign Combinations

CANCER SUN WITH CAPRICORN MOON

You were born around the time of the Full Moon and the blending of these polar opposites in Sun and Moon produces a highly ambitious and determined person, disguised in a mask of friendliness. You are understanding and affectionate and have penetrating insights into human nature. You are well-equipped for a role in the public sector, particularly in politics, and you are likely to gain recognition for your work. Prestige and status are likely to come your way, particularly if you make an effort to achieve them. You have an air of authority about you and always seem willing to assume responsibilities and work hard to reach your goals. You have a natural talent for reassuring people and so they will trust you quite naturally.

Above: you have a natural talent for reassuring people and so they will trust you quite naturally.

Cancer Sun and the 12 Moon Sign Combinations

Because you expect a great deal out of life and appreciate the value of money, you are very likely to be constantly looking for bargains in order to save your precious pennies. You could even go to extremes and become a miser. However, your shrewdness and knowledge of people gives you a genial and warm manner. This is a good blend which allows you to accomplish much without hurting people's feelings. You will gather and retain many close and loyal friends throughout your life. You know how to drive a hard bargain whilst keeping a smile on your face. However, you do have to watch out for going overboard in saving money.

CANCER SUN WITH AQUARIUS MOON

The double fixed combination of your Sun and Moon sign produces an idealistic personality with a great sense of destiny. You are extremely empathic to all types of people. You are able to transmit your understanding of both yourself and others to the people around you. You are only too aware of your own shortcomings and do your utmost to improve yourself. You can put your point of view across to groups and have a talent for making speeches even though you appear detached and aloof. You find one-to-one relationships difficult and not as fulfilling as group work.

Cancer Sun and the 12 Moon Sign Combinations

You appear to be preoccupied and dreamy but this is because you are often dealing with several emotions at the same time. Although you are critical of people it is always well-intentioned as you seek their self-improvement as much as your own. You have a great deal of pride and find it hard to expose your feelings to the people around you. There is nothing petty about you and you have little time for the unkindness of others. You have a natural way of achieving power over others but spend little time or effort making friends. Nevertheless, you are well accepted because of your general concern for the welfare of others. You have a nobility of bearing and attempt to raise people to your level.

Above: you appear to be preoccupied and dreamy but this is because you are often dealing with several emotions at the same time.

Cancer Sun and the 12 Moon Sign Combinations

CANCER SUN WITH PISCES MOON

The double water combination of your Sun and Moon sign gives you the emotional depths of the ocean. You are able to store a constant flow of impressions and you have very accurate instincts. You have a peaceable and gentle personality and rarely get involved in arguments. You are tactful, friendly and agreeable and detest aggression. At times you are so pleasant and amenable that it is hard for others to know where you stand on a subject. This is not to say that you do not have strong viewpoints but you tend to keep them to yourself in case they produce conflict.

You need to develop your self-confidence and be a little more willing to act on your hunches and your intuition. Your ability to apply diplomacy to most situations will ensure your success in most undertakings. You are self-protective, defensive and fairly suspicious of the motives of others. This allows you to protect yourself from predatory people. You have a good business sense and the ability to drive a good bargain. You are naturally drawn to charity work or work with animals or people less fortunate than you. You may also develop your psychic senses and work within the spiritual and self-development fields.

EPILOGUE

Now that you have read this book you may be wondering what use it can be to you. To understand the inner workings of your personality and emotions will allow you to realise your full potential, and astrology is a simple and effective way to achieve this. There is, of course, much more to the subject of astrology than just the Sun and Moon signs. There are all the planets to take into consideration and the houses they fall in. As I said at the beginning, every birth chart is unique, but there are similarities between us all. It is the differences that make us individuals. I hope that in the reading of this book perhaps you will be inspired to look deeper into yourself and deeper into the uses of astrology.

"Know yourself and the truth will set you free"